YOUR KNOWLEDGE HAS VALUE

Imprint:

Copyright © 2015 GRIN Verlag
Print and binding: Books on Demand GmbH, Norderstedt Germany
ISBN: 9783346087607

This book at GRIN:

https://www.grin.com/document/506357

George Yiapanas

Understanding Cross-Cultural Management. The Role of Business Interactions

GRIN Verlag

GRIN - Your knowledge has value

Since its foundation in 1998, GRIN has specialized in publishing academic texts by students, college teachers and other academics as e-book and printed book. The website www.grin.com is an ideal platform for presenting term papers, final papers, scientific essays, dissertations and specialist books.

Visit us on the internet:

http://www.grin.com/

http://www.facebook.com/grincom

http://www.twitter.com/grin_com

University of Wolverhampton
School of Business

MA Management

2015

Understanding cross-cultural management

George Yiapanas
University of Wolverhampton

Introduction

Globalisation refers to the transmission of knowledge, ideas, values, products and services all around the world, shaping a new era of interactions among various political, religious, cultural and economic groups. As a result, it is increasing business interactions between individuals across various geographical and cultural boundaries. Research indicates that companies need to consider cost, availability of skills, environment and quality of infrastructure (Farrell, 2006).

Cross-Border Management

Cross cultural management studies the behaviour of people in organisations all around the world in order to improve communication and interaction (Browaeys & Price, 2011).

Culture is defined as the "characteristics and knowledge of a particular group of people, defined by everything from language, religion, social habits, music and arts" (Zimmermann, 2015). Culture has been compared to an iceberg. Just as an iceberg has a visible section above the waterline and a larger, invisible section below the water line, so culture has some aspects that are observable and others that can only be suspected or imagined. Also like an iceberg, the part of culture that is visible is only a small part of a much bigger whole (Storti and Bennhold-Samaan, 1997).

"Management in its broadest sense consists of the co-ordination of the efforts of people and the use of economic and technical resources in order to obtain desired ends" (Hofstede, 1984). According to Holden (2002), it must be related to managerial activity in the new geo-economy with its emphasis on global networking, organisational learning and knowledge management. It is very crucial for cross-border management to collect relevant information and gain knowledge about specific situations that companies need, but misjudge, miss, or generally lack access to.

Offshoring refers to the delegation of services in another country and it could be done by either creating an internal entity or through outsourcing to a foreign contractor. Lohr (2004) defined offshoring and offshore outsourcing as "the migration of jobs and operators to lower-cost countries".

The external service provider actually takes care of hiring and training all the employees, maintains the software and infrastructure and runs the day to day operations. Selecting the outsourcing solution, generally, involves a trade-off between either the benefit of a low cost external solution and the loss of managerial control over the process. Loss of control may be a problem when employees lack company knowledge and they are not familiar the company's products, services, practices and its customers' culture.

In order to secure high level services, a contract should be signed, spesifying the fees, the duration and the obligations of each party etc. According to Jensen and Meckling (1995), contracting is a means to guarantee the fulfilment of the obliations of each party and the effectiveness of contracts may depend on the ability of partners to measure the quality and quantity of services.

One of the main advantages of offshoring is achieving lower costs associated with operation expenses, infrastructure, overheads and labour" (Collier & Evans, 2009). In addition to the above, it allows companies to have tax savings (Vogel & Connolly, 2005).

The most crucial obstacle when offshoring is the communication. Cross-Cultural communication occurs when a person from one culture sends a message to a person from another culture. "Miscommunications occur when the person from one culture does not receive the message" (Adler, 1991). Lack in communication skills may lead to miscommunication and cause frustration to the clients (Flatworld, 2015). Accent neutralisation is not enough and it is not easy to teach cultural awareness. Some have criticised that, "all too often, attempts at mimicking a foreign culture fall flat. An appreciation of the style and culture of a foreign land cannot be learned through a process of television osmosis" (Kobayashi-Hillary, 2004). Most third-party employees are constantly struggling to adapt and improve their accent. They are also encouraged to study the culture and lifestyle of the visiting company in an attempt to understand their customers and learn about significant events in that geographical location. Only after successfully completing this initial training would product training begin (Das et al, 2008).

Edward Hall's theory of high-low context culture helps us understand better the powerful effect culture has on communication. The key factor in his theory is context and "cultures are compared on a scale from high to low context" (Hall & Hall, 1990). "This relates to the framework, background, and surrounding circumstances in which communication or an event takes place" (Hall, 1977).

High Context	**Low Context**
A high context culture values formality, face-saving communication, relationships and the slower pace needed to develop relationships	A low context culture values informality, direct communication, results, fast pace and punctuality
<ul><li>Conduct business through development of relationships</li><li>Nonverbal communication is important</li><li>Contracts are the basis of relationships</li><li>Time is fluid and schedules tend to be flexible</li></ul>	<ul><li>Relationships interfere with business</li><li>Precise verbal agreements re important</li><li>Contracts are binding and exists apart from personal relationships</li><li>Time is treated as a commodity and schedules are carefully observed</li></ul>

In high context cultures internal meaning is usually embedded deep in the information, so not everything is explicitly stated in writing or when spoken. The listener is expected to be able to read 'between the lines', to understand the unsaid, thanks to his or her background knowledge (Hall, 1977). In low context cultures meanings are explicitly stated through language. People usually expect explanations when something remains unclear. As Hall (1977) explains, "most information is expected to be in the transmitted message in order to make up for what is missing in the context". People assign meaning to a message according to their cultural context.

High level context cultures rely less on verbal communication, while low level cultures the exact opposite and this could create misunderstandings. The explicitness with which they communicate can often cause offence and resentment (Flatworld, 2015).

Most of the times, the visiting country provides a round the clock service as operations are performed in different time zones and this increases the efficiency of the company (Vogel & Connolly, 2005). On the other hand, shift hours interfere with family relationships as employees do not spend significant time with their families and friends and they become isolated (Mohan, 2011).

Religion is an important organising principle, around which people define their identity (Das et al, 2008). Some religion practices include daily rituals and recitations which may affect operations if management does not take religion diversity into consideration.

Stereotypes are generalisations that may or may not be factual and often overlook real, deeper differences. They basically involve categorising and making perceptions about people based on experiences and guide their behaviour towards that group of people in a particular way. Most stereotypes usually tend to convey a negative impression. "When members of stereotyped groups are aware of negative stereotypes about them, they may fear that others will apply these negative qualities to them. These thoughts may be anxiety-provoking and lead to lower performance" (Schneider, 2005).

Corporate social responsibility (CSR) refers to a business practice that involves participating in initiatives that benefit the society. The main important drivers of CSR are: environment and pollution, ecological sustainability, waste, natural resource depletion, climate change and the increasing of the CSR discussion and heighten expectations for proactive corporate action (Werther and Chandler, 2013). This way, the company will differentiate in the market, cut costs and earn public trust. Companies should focus on CSR strategy and become a driver of its development by treating employees fairly and ethically. They must develop CSR standards and objectives for the employees, maintain a training program on a frequent basis about CSR principles and keep a daily communication and close relations with the visiting country management (Werther and Chandler, 2013).

Companies might face various ethical dilemmas during their offshore operations. Ethics describes a generally accepted set of moral principles. It is a code of behaviour that a society considers moral and appropriate for guiding relationship with one another. "Ethics involves judgment as to good and bad, right and wrong and what ought to be" (Hartman, 2002). This could be a possible hazard while contracting an offshore cooperation.

One of the biggest ethical dilemma that may occur, concerns the working environment. Employees are often "subject to extreme exploitation, including the absence of a living wage or benefits, poor working conditions, and arbitrary discipline, such as verbal and physical abuse" (Ramishvili, 2012). Defenders of sweatshops often bring up the fact that even though sweatshops are bad, they at least give people jobs they would not have had otherwise.

However, the types of salaries sweatshop workers receive are so bad that they rarely improve their economic situation. In order to avoid any "uncomfortable" situations, companies should include specific guidelines, and environmental standards in the contract, but there is always the possibility to come across legal matters, ethical dilemmas, corruption and bribery that will have to be solved in a decisive way.

Companies should establish and maintain relations with the offshore management and formulate a team structure and roles. According to Belbin (1981), team roles are used to identify people's behavioural strengths and weaknesses in the workplace. This information can be used to build productive working relationships, select and develop high-performing teams, raise self-awareness and personal effectiveness and build mutual trust and understanding.

However, some of the risks that companies may face include damaging their reputation, customer dissatisfaction and reduced brand loyalty (Sharma et al., 2009). Cultural differences have an impact and the larger the difference the greater the impact on customer satisfaction (Hutzschenreuter et al., 2011).

Cultural Dimensions

Culture is linked to particular groups based on various factors, including geography, ethnicity, age, gender, language, occupation etc. The term "culture" lacks a consensual agreement among social scientists (Alas et al., 2008). One common definition comes from Geert Hofstede (1984) who defines culture as "the collective programming of the mind which distinguishes the members of one category of people from those of another".

According to Hofstede (1983a), cultural dimensions describe the effects of a society's culture on the values of its members and how these values relate to behaviour, using a structure derived from factor analysis. Hofstede developed his original model as a result of using factor analysis to examine the results of a world-wide survey in the 1970s.

The original theory proposed four dimensions:

1. Low vs. High power distance
2. Individualism vs. collectivism
3. Masculinity vs. Femininity
4. Low vs. High uncertainty avoidance

A fifth dimension was added in the 2000s based on research by Michael Minkov, using data from the World Values Survey, while a sixth dimension followed based on Hofstede and Minkov's analysis. Both dimensions are supported by Hofstede, as he analysed a large database of employee value scores in more than 70 countries and ranked each country according to its culture (Hofstede, 2011).

The fifth and sixth dimensions are:

5. Short-Term vs. Long-Term orientation
6. Indulgence vs. Restraint

Low vs. High power distance

Power distance dimension deals with the fact that all individuals are not equal and describes the desire for hierarchy. "It is the extent to which the members of a society accept that power in institutions and organisations is distributed unequally" (Hofstede, 1984b). People in large power distance societies accept a hierarchical order in which everybody has a place which needs no further justification while people in small power distance societies strive for power equalisation and demand justification for power inequalities among people when they occur.

High power culture have big gaps between the week and the powerful, have an appreciation for hierarchy in the organisation, they depend on the management or the power holder and they do not question the decisions of their leaders. "They are given less opportunity for discretion and problem solving while under high levels of surveillance" (Das et al, 2008).

Managers earn more money and respect and they count on the obedience of their team members. Employees expect to be directed clearly as to their functions and what is expected of them. Communication is top down but often feedback which is negative is never offered up the ladder. According to Youngdahl et al. (2010), "employees who exhibit high power distance usually are reluctant to seek expertise or opinions from superiors".

Low power distance	High power distance
There should be a minimum of inequality since it can exploit others	Inequality is unavoidable and everyone has the place they disserve
If there is a hierarchy in an organisation it is only for the sake of convenience	Hierarchy in an organisation reflects natural differences
People who are superiors or subordinates are the same	Superiors or subordinates are different kinds of people
Everyone should enjoy the same privileges; there should be no symbols	Power-holders are entitled to privileges and status-symbols
Sub ordinaries should be consulted	Sub ordinaries should be told what to do
Individuality is to be respected	Authority is to be respected
The manager should be a resourceful democrat	The manager should be a benevolent autocrat

Individualism vs. Collectivism

Individualism's fundamental issue is the degree of independence a society maintains among its members. "It stands for a preference for a loosely knit social framework in society wherein individuals are supposed to take care of themselves and their immediate family only. Its opposite, collectivism, stands for a preference for a tightly knit social framework in which individuals can expect their relatives or other in-group to look after them in exchange for unquestioning loyalty. I relates to people's self-concept: 'I' or 'We' "(Hofstede, 1984b).

In individualistic societies, each person emphasises on his or her own self-interest, decisions are based primarily on individual needs and tasks prevail over relationships, whether in collectivist societies, people belong to groups that take care of them in exchange for loyalty, decisions are primarily made according to what is the best for the group and relationships prevail over task.

The collectivist side indicates that the employees have a high preference for belonging to a larger social framework in which individuals are expected to act in accordance to the greater good of a greater group. This means that their actions are according to the influence of various

4

concerns, such as their family, their friends and their work group. There is loyalty between employees and management and hiring and promotion decisions are made based on relationships (Das et al, 2008).

In an effective team, each employee knows he (or she) depends on others for achieving his/her final result, which means that team members have an interest in helping each other where they can. This could work as a benefit, since everyone will work for the good of the whole group and not for their own benefit. This can produce more efficiency which will increase productivity and performance. It could also develop their skills and help identify their strengths and weaknesses. The key point on this aspect is to ensure that recruitments are made with high standards and specific requirements (Hofstede, 1984b).

The individualistic side means that the employees' decisions are based primarily on their individual need and they focus on individual initiative and achievement. This could easily lead to efficiency and productivity problems which will cause weaknesses in the company. Companies need to ensure with management that the production or service remains on high levels and the agents focus on their duties with loyalty despite their personal needs (Das et al, 2008).

Collectivist	Individualist
'We' mentality	'I' mentality
Identity is based on one's social group	Identity is based on the individual
Decisions are primarily made according to what is best for the group	Decisions are based primarily on individual needs
Relationships prevail over task	Tasks prevail over relationships
Focus is on belongings to an organisation	Focus is on individual initiative and achievement
Values differ according to the group (particularism)	Value standards apply to all (universalism)

Masculinity vs. Femininity

The masculinity - femininity dimension measures the preference for sex-role distinctions to be made between men and women in a particular culture. "It stands for a preference in society for achievement, heroism, assertiveness, and material success. Its opposite, Femininity, stands for a preference for relationships, modesty, caring for the weak, and the quality of life" (Hofstede, 1984b). Such societies become 'welfare societies' in which caring for all members, even the weakest, is an important goal for men as well as women.

Masculine cultures value competitiveness, ambition, achievement and success, the accumulation of wealth, people live to work, they have sympathy for the achiever and managers are expected to be decisive and assertive. Feminine cultures emphasise nurturing roles, interdependence among people, and caring for less fortunate people - both men and women (Hofstede, 1984b).

Masculinity	Femininity
Distinct gender roles	Fluid gender roles
Men are assertive, women are nurturing	Men and women in nurturing roles
Stress on competition and performance	Stress on co-operation and environmental awareness
Acquisition of wealth	Quality of life
Ambition motivates	Service motivates
Live to work	Work to live
Sympathy for successful achiever	Sympathy for the unfortunate
Managers are expected to be decisive and assertive	Managers use intuition and strive for consensus

Low vs. High uncertainty avoidance

The Uncertainty Avoidance dimension has to do with the way that a society deals with the fact that the future can never be known. Hofstede (1984b) believes that the uncertainty avoidance impacts the meaning of time and the desire for precision and punctuality.

High uncertainty avoidance societies create institutions to minimise risk and ensure security. They are ready to take risks, they have fewer rules, deviance is not a threat to them, and they take things as they come. On the other hand, in low uncertainty avoidance societies, managers are relatively entrepreneurial and comfortable with risk. They are concerned with security, they resist to changes and believe that uncertainty in life is a threat and must be reduced (Hofstede, 1984b).

Low uncertainty avoidance	High uncertainty avoidance
Uncertainty in life is threatening and must be reduced	Uncertainty is a fact of life. Take things as they come
Intolerant of deviant persons and ideas	Deviance is not a threat
Predictability and clarity are preferable	Ambiguity is tolerant
Concern about security	Readiness to take risks
Resistance to change	Toleration of innovation
Formal rules and regulations are necessary	The fewer the rules there are the better
Consensus is better than conflict	Competition an conflict can be constructive
Belief in experts and their knowledge	Belief in generalists and common sense

Indulgence vs. Restraint

Indulgence dimension stands for a society that allows or not relatively free gratification of basic and natural human drives related to enjoying life and having fun. This dimension identifies the "extent to which a society allows relatively free gratification of basic and natural human desires related to enjoying life and having fun," as represented by the 'indulgence' point on the continuum, relative to a society that controls gratification of needs and regulates by means of strict social norms" (Hofstede, 2011).

Restraint cultures control gratification of needs and regulate it by means of strict social norms. Indulgence societies are relatively free regarding the basic human desires, such as personal life control, participation in sports, freedom of speech, etc. while restrained societies place low importance on leisure, freedom of speech is not a primary concern and only few people are actively involved in sports.Restraint culture employees might have a tendency to cynicism and pessimism and feel that indulging themselves is somewhat wrong.

Indulgence	Restrained
Higher percentage of people declaring themselves very happy	Fewer very happy people
A perception of personal life control	A perception of helplessness. What happens to me is not my own doing
Freedom of speech seen important	Freedom of speech is not a primary concern
Higher importance of leisure	Lower importance of leisure
More likely to remember positive emotions	Less likely to remember positive emotions
In countries with educated populations, higher birth-rates	In countries with educational populations, lowers birtrates
More people actively involved in sports	Fewer people actively involved in sports
In countries with enough food, higher percentages of obese people	In countries with enough food, fewer obese people
In wealthy countries, lenient sexual norms	In wealthy countries, stricter sexual norms

Limitations

Although Hofstede's dimensions have been widely accepted, his framework suffers from some limitations. His study was based on data collected from 1968 to 1972, the framework fails to account for the convergence of cultural values, his findings are based on the employees of a single company (IBM) and the data were collected using questionnaires.

Some critics suggest that the number of dimensions should be expanded and dimensions should not be reified. They do not 'exist' in a tangible sense (Levitin, 1973).

The future technological advances might strongly influence culture changes and lead to partly similar changes in different cultures, but on the other hand, technology might increase differences on the basis of pre-existing technological and cultural differentiations.

In response to these limitations Fons Trompenaars developed a new study model which explains the significance of managerial value within cross-cultural practices. The model was based on a ten-year research on the preferences and values of people in many cultures around the world (Trompenaars and Hampden-Turner, 1997). He concluded that what distinguishes people from one culture compared with people from another culture is where these preferences fall in one of his seven dimensions.

Adler (1991) defined these problems as individual interpretations that exist at the level of values, and that determine human behaviour. Adler gives six dimensions that we can use to analyse cultural differences.

Conclusion

Literature shows that cultural differences have an impact and the larger the difference the greater the impact on customer satisfaction. The implications are that there are differences in work-related values in different countries and an understanding of these differences is needed to develop appropriate strategies.

Companies considering offshoring their call centre should contemplate location choices on the basis of national culture distance to minimise the compatibility conflicts. It is very critical to choose the offshoring that fits their brand, not just their price point and understand the culture of the country they are doing business in. Companies should maintain relations and establish mutual trust with the call centre management, formulate a team structure and roles, secure the quality of communication, enforce data security measures and specify the codes of ethics and morals.

It is in the benefit of the company to evaluate the decision to offshore, on an a regular basis, relying on the information collected from their customers and employees. Without this knowledge, a successful outcome could be in jeopardy. Such sensible decisions should not be taken only based on pure financial strategic reasons.

Companies should acquire factual and interpretive knowledge, avoid cultural bias and develop cross-cultural skills. Cultural compatibility needs to be considered to ensure that companies' customers will enjoy high quality products or services.

References

Alas R, Kaarelson T, and Niglas K (2008) *Human Resource Management in cultural context: Empirical study of 11 countries*. EBS Review

Adler, N. (1991) *International Dimensions of Organizational Behavior*. 2nd Ed. Boston, MA: PWS-KENT Publishing Company

Alster, N. (2005) *Customer disservice?*

Belbin, M. (1981) *Management Teams*. London: Heinemann

Browaeys, M. & Price, R. (2011) Understanding Cross-cultural Management, 2nd Ed: Pearson Education

Collier, D. and Evans, J. (2009*) OM² - Offshoring* (pp. 31-33)

Das, Diya, Dharwadkar, Brandes, Pamela. (2008) *The importance of being 'Indian': Identity centrality and work outcomes in an off - shored call center in India*. Human Relations, 61(11), 1499-1530

Deterding, S., Khaled, R., Nacke, L. E., & Dixon, D (2011) *CHI 2011*, May 7–12, 2011, Vancouver, BC, Canada.

Farell, D. (2006) *Smarter offshoring*. Harvard Business Review, pp. 85-92

Flatworld Solutions (2015) *The Benefits of Call Ceter Outsourcing*. [online]. [Accessed 22 Mar 2015].

Hall, E. (1977) *Beyond Culture*. Edition. Anchor Books.

Hall, E. & Hall, M. (1990) *Understanding cultural differences: Germans, French and Americans*. Yarmouth: Intercultural Press.

Hartman, L. P. (2002) *Perspectives in Business Ethics*. 2nd ed, New York: McGraw-Hill

Hofstede, G (1983a) *"Dimensions of National Cultures in Fifty Countries and Three Regions"* in *Expiscations in Cross-Cultural Psychology*. Netherlands: Swets & Zeitlinger.

Hofstede, G. (1984) *The cultural relativity of the quality of life concept*. Academy of Management Review, 9 (3).

Hofstede, G. (1984b) *"Cultural Dimensions in Management and Planning"*, *Asia Pacific*. Journal of Management, January, pp. 81-99.

Hofstede, G. (1993) *Hofstede's Research on Cross-Cultural Work-Related Values: Implications for Consumer Behaviour*.

Hofstede, G. (2003) Culture's Consequences: Comparing Values, Behaviors, Institutions and Organizations Across Nations. 2nd Edition. SAGE Publications, Inc.

Hofstede, G. (2011) *Dimensionalizing cultures: The Hofstede model in context*.

Holden. N. (2002) *Cross-cultural Management. A Knowledge Management Approach*, Perspective: Pearson Education

Hutzschenreuter T, Lewin AY and Dresel S (2011) *Time to success in offshoring business processes: A multi-level analysis*. Management International Review

Jensen, M. C., & Meckling, W. H. (1995) *Specific and General Knowledge, and Organizational Structure*.Journal of Applied Corporate Finance, pp. 4-18

Kobayashi-Hillary M. (2004) *Outsourcing to India: The offshore advantage*. Berlin: Springer.

Levitin, T. (1973) *Values. In J. P. Robinson & P. R. Shaver (Eds.), Measures of social psychological attitudes* (pp. 489-502). Ann Arbor, MI: University of Michigan, Institute for Social Research, Survey Research Center.

Lohr, S. (2004) *Many new causes for old problems of jobs lost abroad*. New York Times.

Markus, H. R., & Kitayama, S. (1991) *Culture and the self: Implications for cognition, emotion, and motivation*. Psychological review. pp.224-253

Mohan, K. (2011) *Cultural values and globalization: India's dilemma*. Current Sociology, pp. 214-228

Murphy, J. (2011) *Indian call centre workers: vanguard of a global middle class? Work, Employment & Society*, pp. 417-433

Ramishvili, T. (2012). *Sweatshops and child labour: The price of fashion?*

Sharma P, Mathur R and Dhawan A (2009) *Exploring customer reactions to offshore call centers: Toward a comprehensive conceptual framework*. The Journal of Services Marketing.

Shneider, D. (2005) *The Philosophy of Stereotyping*. The Guilford Press

Storti, C. and Bennhold-Samaan, L. (1997) *Culture matters*. Washington, DC: Peace Corps Information Collection and Exchange, p. 10.

Trompenaars, F and Hampden-Turner, C. (1997) *Riding The Waves of Culture: Understanding Diversity in Global Business*. 2nd Edition. McGraw-Hill.

Vogel, D. and Connolly, E. (2005) *Best Practices for Dealing with Offshore Software Development*.

Youngdahl W, Ramaswamy K. and Dash K. (2010) *Service offshoring: The evolution of offshore operations*. International Journal of Operations & Production Management, pp. 798-820.

Werther, W. and Chandler, D. (2013) *"Strategic Corporate Social Responsibility"*. Sage Publications

Zimmernmann, K. (2015) *What is Culture. Definition of Culture.*

YOUR KNOWLEDGE HAS VALUE